My Pen Bleeds

A fire keeps burning

Sany Sayantanee

Contents

1

Odd Duck

Outlandish and alone he is, so what..!
Can stand rock-like, all by himself.
Nonpareil may be he, to fellows around,
Thats what makes him different.
Sheeps in flocks are seen far and near.
The bigotry mindsets by and large.
To align with the majority,
To access the comfort zone.
Even if all it means, stampede..suffocation.
They who accredit fakeness to genuineness,
And endorse and count on fugitive wealth.
Sans any concern for the dishevelled, downtrodden,
With indifference cast their eyes off them.
A salute to the maverick, his prodigy,
His solemn thoughts of dissent.
Who knows when to split away from orthodoxy,
When to assemble for nobility.
Per se, he is that alchemist,
The one who has mastered quite many things,
And above all the art of introvert living.
That from the gravest of his injuries,
He came out to be the kindest of souls.
Penetrated deep..the rumoured,
much feared, forbidden land of solitude.
And tasted the succulent heavenly fruits there, nowhere else be found.

2

Horizon

Horizons are illusory, deceptive, ever shifting.

The seemingly rendezvous of the sky with the earth.

Our world should not be cut off there,

For the sun and the moon, rise and sink beyond them.

Eternity cannot be defined in terms of boundaries.

When the nebulous haze surrounds you.. Your vision is blurred, the horizon, obscured.

For adventurers or trailblazers its ever changing.

If you are looking out for respite, look beyond the horizons.

For in infinity lies hopes, possibilities.

As you move on, in life you see a new sun..a new moon,

And your horizon is not the same again.

Know then..its not the horizon, but your perception, your position.

A self-introspection

History of Todays, I revisited.
Many a slaughtered hopes I found.
Slain at the altar of false pride.
Some draped in vainglory, in the name of providence.
Still some enslaved by the wistful desires.
Some blinded by the floodlight of outward glamour.
In the fruition of a vague, abstract futuristic thought..
How come I overlooked, the empowered 'Now'.
This day that holds everything per se..
To curb the progradation of fatal innermost foes..
And build bridges of warmth galore..
To stitch the torns, embalm the burns..
And waste not emotions, haste not life..
To stir life in me with acceptance..
And sow and grow the seeds of love.

4

Love beyond borders

Love transcends, frontiers of alienating acrimony.
With wide open wings embraces heartily the sky.
Casting a pitiful eye on prisoners of golden cages.
And on those bloodshed man-acclaimed territories.
A bridge that connects two beautiful souls.
The traffic of rushing emotions ceaselessly flow.
Those narrow bends of stagnant minds lag behind.
Only the fearless, brave hearts march ahead of all.
A river that has never given up to an obstacle.
Must incise through steadily to make its way.
So miserably yearns for the Sea to meet and deliver.
With a heavenly kiss to loose itself in namelessness.
The earth too shakes and not a thing stands.
The tallest of walls crumble, collapse and fall.
To pave the path for sacred glory to emerge.
And build an edifice out of bricks of love.
The unsurmountable ranges of majestic mounts.
Where perseverance turns the odds to evens.
Those terrains are now warm and welcoming.
To scale the staggering heights but one must climb.
Oh!! the divine air how knows of the hidden fire.
Carries the immersed thoughts of the beloved.
Frame of mind as of telepathy is read.
Two distant hearts synchronously beat.
Name it love or sacrifice...love and you're no more mortal.

The invincible in me

How come ye perceive me when I haven't explored my interior?

Who can say a minor fault can break the asthenosphere!

Do not be mistaken by what you find,

May be it's your cynical delusion.

I'm just not a lone voice,

But the voice of all those men, women.

Then demolish me, subdue my voice,

Find me again in thousand ways.

Cremate me if you can,

I bet shall rise above the ashes.

How you forethought the night would hide the dark of your deeds!

How could it be when the night too has eyes and to the Sun it leads!

6

Until death do us part

You're my zephyr, I'm your petrichor.

You're the Yin , I'm the Yang.

As we blend, miracles happen.

How you laminated my life with the light of your love!

How my passionate soul is blessed, my heart only knows!

Bonded though we are for life, love evolves, metamorphoses.

In this peregrination, goes through trials and vicissitudes.

Love redefines itself once and again..for us to scale new heights.

My beloved! Every day is not a rosy day with pink love in the air.

Sometimes its thorny, sometimes it pricks and really hurts.

The sun and the rain could make beautiful rainbows, together we can.

In this endeavour, our cornerstones be love, patience and commitment.

We learn as we grow, discern things that are detrimental and that make it.

Let's make this journey an adventure.

Let's make our mission possible.

And face the ups and downs of life with hugs and kisses.

Adversaries, be it sickness, misfortune can never win over us.

Not distance and not time can part us but a transitory death.

A Lotus growth

A sheen of pink aglow, bloomed out of its buried dark.

Spurred to prove, its self worth from reality so stark.

Takes off from the murky mud, to symbolise enlightenment..

To reflect a pure, composed, discerning mind's attainment.

Out of the clutches of samsara that stagnates spiritual growth...

Its reeds take her up higher, through awake, arise to rebirth.

Seeks for the path of abolute truth, devotion, deliverance by the way of renunciation.

Relieves from the tangled worldly pleasures or sufferings to the soul's emancipation.

8

Romancing Coffee...

'twas a thought-out plan to entice me with unadulterated love..
And gladden the day's hectic workloads, thumping head.
A secret coffee was brewing in a tango dance mode.
Coffee and sweetened milk moved hands entwined.
Mischievous air knew it.. escaped to spread.
Aroma of coffee lingered through my senses.
Pianissimo rain created the right ambience.
I set off ruminating with a gripping ardent desire...
The enriching, authentic flavour to savour my palette.
Couldn't make out who was more eager...coffee or me!
It covered the whole distance to come into my warm hold.
I fetched the mug of steaming hot coffee like a true lover.
Inhaled it's spiralled yearnings to reach my driven heart.
Impassioned...still slackened, afraid of scalding the lingo.
Soothingly osculated at brief hiatuses.
Eyes furled inwards to feel the inner bliss.
Moods uplifted, I landed on cloud nine.
Casted off the worn-out, wearisome frame...
Entered a newer version of me, revitalised.

9

Common Crow

The shrill and rough 'caw' speaks with pain in the voice.
When looked down upon, can they cry a cuckoo?
Their desperate cawing fall into deaf years.
People often forget their unfelt existence.
Eyes drawn to parrots, canaries, kingfishers.
The plebians are never ever paid attention.
Yet they have been cawing in the same coarse tone..
Through generations, across ages, civilizations.
We grow with common crows from childhood.
Monuments, temples, bridges, towering buildings..
Elegant edifices stand tall as a symbol of their blood 'n sweat.
Dedicated hands growing food grains, veggies, edibles...
They are the ones sustaining millions, satiating hunger.
Toiling day and night to make garments...
They are the ones cladding us with clothes.
The shapers of great civilizations...
For them the wheels of life keeps rolling.
They are the amazing creators, next to God.
Factory workers, peasants, building labourers and the like.
Their work is no less significant yet they are anonymous.
They are mishandled, overlooked and forgotten.
The prestige and recognition which they rightfully deserve..
Wrongfully bestowed upon kings, and the rulling class.
The privileges are bestowed to elites and bureaucrats.
They pass away sans honour, unknown, unacknowledged.

10

Kintsugi

Then when our hearts were merged into one.
Ifs and buts challenged us and we overcame.
Cryptic quietude was easy to decipher.
That simple it was to simplify the puzzles.
Anyways they would unify into a jig saw fit.
Now at the crossroads why that dilemma!
Hijacked emotions overtaking poor me.
Why some pieces seem to go missing..!
A large many mismatch or I forgot to play?
How I wish I could bring them together as ere.
Would spend my last fortune to make it happen.
I have strong faith around where love mends.
Kintsugi is real...gold seams beautify evermore.

Life and Afterlife

Here it is life, vibrant..undulating breaths go ceaseless.
There it is death, life captured to flow elsewhere.
An ethereal bubble of life, bagged with myriad aspirations.
A realm of afterlife, unknown, may be bereft of desires.
Enigmas of life, afterlife form a cycle of Karmas, pluses, minuses.
The anastomosing channels, flowing one to the other.
A connecting space, the transit regulate Stop-and-Go.
The chain will break some fateful day perhaps...
As the soul cleared of impurities reaches its perfection...
To mingle with the omnipotent oneness, the constant.
Till then it must surpass the intricate process..
The earthly attachment followed by detachment...
Of emotions that bind and then abruptly that fleet.
A play it is, when it's over, one must return the serene abode.
We all are essentially the same, playing different roles.
Intriguing the dark matter has every mystery in its fold.
The infinite vacuity enveloping is in real all-encompassing.
And human cognizance is overrated with having a discerning mind.
Now I know..I am simply lifeless, nonentity, just an immaterial thought.

12

Poetry never dies

In divine disposition it reincarnates..
With its appearance and reappearance.
Indestructible, infinite, all pervasive...
Static or dynamic in the cosmos it remains.
Almighty's the generator.
A bard's but a propagator.
Cognition dissipates with earthen frames, revives again.
Sparks of unitary God pass them on to recur in cyclic chain.
Methinks..Having exhausted my alloted existing hour...
When the decayed organics would be lost to the thin air...
Withdrawn though yet would happen to be there...
As thoughts would reinstate in starry eyes pair.
Beats and breaths would be the reader's.
Blisses and blues may give out wonders.
Someone somewhere reading out would kindle a fire.
Would I then sense them all wherever I may retire.
My Poesies would breathe again to life as words reverberate.
My long silenced Poems would rise from a moribund state.

13

Cheer up to the blues

The intruders boom into your haven as unwelcomed guests.
Unexpectedly, unreasonably turn up from nowhere all at once.
Some dormant phases do come to sojourn such a way.
At times you can't help, rather learn to bear with it.
An entangled labyrinth of gossamer trap.
And a restless spider caught in its own web.
A turtle overturned underneath its tough protective shell.
The shield that saved its breaths till now becomes useless.
It's when your sky is grey, dismal for days together...
And the sun missing out, fails to pay you a visit.
You may be giving out your right arm in vain...
Pushing hard to boost your inept senses.
Just that..things won't work the way you wish.
The outcomes of labour would be horribly harrowing .
With meagre you would then learn to suffice.
Crawl through your setbacks with snail's pace.
Sometimes it do happen...
And it happens with everyone.
Curse not your fate, count not yourself fragile.
A star you are..have burnt your core many a times.
And evolved with a much denser core each time.
Have made it time and again with renewed grit.
It's time to caress...Give it a break.
Let all thoughts subside and calmness pervade.
Sleep, meditate..lend your soul a rest to rejuvenate.
Your Ikigai will await your sheweth.
With a suave of unhindered smoothness, akin to the avians..
Yet again you'll glide across the clouds of your imagination.

Mystic

Beyond the human intellect, an occult enigma transcends.
The seven Kalas converged here, to be named ' the Illuminati'.
Absolute grace and charisma, nimbus surrounding divinity .
Effulgent aura captivates, dissociate all earthly concerns.
Magnetic reverberation takes one in entirety, overwhelms.
A forceful whirlpool that pulls in the body, mind and soul.
That navel of absolute truth, confides the mystery of life.
There surrender the self in devotional love, immerse in ecstasy.

All my sons and daughters

The orb was spitting out flares of ire remorselessly.
Half-fed, half-naked, half-loved kids in the fore front.
Not to brave it..instead to gamble their stars.
Sloth-pace they moved in the fast forward life.
Non conformal to the updated, organised world.
Despair looming under their darkened sockets.
The rising treacherous pangs, let alone a morsel.
Yet all the same guilelessness in their calm eyes..
I felt..My very own children bereft of love and care.
For me they looked akin..just the same way it touched.
How could I have side tracked and parted away!
I peeped into my soul to find an ocean of warmth.
Breaking the barriers, made a world of difference.
The motherhood in me rose to new dimensions.
Aren't they my beloved sons and daughters!

Apocalyptic Debacle

Relapse following resilience and the cycle goes on.
Hopes devastated of a vulnerable section.
That frail, fragile structure, that pale-faced, sunburnt mass.
Sweltering, palpitating, soiled, fatigued.. toiling breathless.
Every cell giving up..still, holding on to the last resort.
Persevering, he manoeuvres his umpteenth effort.
The sunken, half-fed eyes of his children, he feeds a million mouths.
Unscrupulous greed has no end..
The vicious predators suck on his life blood manifold.
To hell with inclusiveness..even unnoticed are they,
Their overwhelming numbers and fate goes the same.
This shameless power play game seems to have no end!
Existentialism is disproved, pawns sacrificed first.
Lo! How rudimentary is he!
His dreams barely go beyond his plot of land, perchance.
Stiffened by hardships untold, he smiles not always,
But when his golden paddy fields dance.
A friend to nature..Yet bears the brunts, the impacts of severity and why?
They blame it on the Industrial-Nuclear age..
The ravaging cyclones, floods and droughts.
And unassessed, unrecognised lie his crop failures..
Viscous poverty, malady and encumbering debts.
Name it a man made disaster, a heinous crime, a death trap..
Undercurrent of inequation runs..widening the marxian gap.

Sorry state of affairs

Oops!! That globular glass paper weight falls yet again..
Like some bomb dropped..breaks the pin drop silence..
Selectively at the library, common room, office..
Prying eyes on me, I smile abashed, elusively escape.
That full glass of water carried with utmost care..
With a crab's firm grip and spider's determination.
Still somehow..somehow mischievously slips off..
Poor soul with thirsty eyes gape at my blunder.
I wonder why it alone, always happens with me..
Awkward catastrophic situations arise out of nowhere.
My umbrella turns a parachute, everyone else's is fine.
And I stumble very often..with or without an obstacle.
I think to myself am I loosing friction with the earth!
They say I live in my dreamworld and need to be pragmatic.
Sandals love my sweat of embarassment, kill my trust half away.
Bewildered me, bare feet I amble as if I'm a pious soul on pilgrim.
Garments, torn by that lurking culprit nail as I swipe by it..
And see I am to be blamed without sense..say where is my fault!
'Misplaced' has become my hackneyed catch word..
Documents actually go for a refreshing outing..
At times return late and at others get lost in the open air.

Labyrinth of mind

Hellbound I'm..pulled and pushed out of proportion.
So desperate this sordid state, tethered to the fate.
No chance of respite from the cycle of misery.
As if the venom awaits and awaits only to be gulped by me.
My own mind plays foul against me, whom to expect!
Smiles are but debts, must be payed with an interest.
When pains call me, must move at once, can't help it.
Knowing all..I myself approach the death trap.
Left with no choice I enter the goblet of fire.
There my soul is blazed of encircling abhorrence.
Half burnt it returns to its heaven to douse in solace.
But then again pain sirens and the soul is dragged.
No relief from its sinister gripping claws.
I restlessly swing between hell and paradise.
No where I'm a consistent resident..no where I live.
Lost in the intriguing maze of life with blocked roads.
Someday perse the evil force will have no influence.
A karma will end and seraphims will be omnipotent.

It's never...'The End'

If you have misgivings about life..
Having found unfounded relationships.
If you are left forlorn with your wounds..
The worst you feel and loose your grips.
If there is blinding darkness all around..
If you don't find a ray of light or sound.
Then be sure, it's not the ultimate end..
But soon a dawn to appear my friend.
The game in entirety is not over.
Hold on a bit you are not a loser.
If you have not a choice to opt for and strive.
If you do not have worth a cause to be alive.
If you accuse fate for deceptively playing on your emotions so long.
If you are despised by closest people for justifiably doing no wrong.
It's never a mindless game, or a cake walk..it's the game of life..
Why not give the umpteenth efforts,
Transcend above pains, strife!
May you then play to the fullest.
Play harder at full blast.
Play with passion as best as you can.
Play as a great enthusiast.
If the prevailing foggy conditions prevent you from a far sight.
If your body, soul on the verge to surrender is not set for a fight.
If from inside you are fed up with a feigned life and fallacious pride.
If you have suffered to the nth degree and the agony still you hide.
Whatever it is, don't you ever give up.

Steadily the fortitude may you build up.

Wait with all your patience, till what is dark, light.

Make the most of time, till what is wrong, be right.

Inasmuch as there is always a light for a way.

And so also there is always a way for a will.

If you are aimlessly drifting..try hard regurgitate that vile.

If the path seems endless, be steadfast, cover that extra mile.

If your mind is much agitated..take time, be self-composed.

Creep and crawl so that you may walk.

And go on walking, till you run atlast.

Mind's the open sky

Albeit a frame of flesh and blood is that simple to captivate...
Can be confined or caged, tethered or enslaved.
The indomitable mind knows not to yield to terms.
It's transcendental, boundless.. the heaven, its haven.
Gives not an ear to the hellbound satanic dictates.
But to the lilting heart, a vista to realise its dreams.
Divulges vehemently...'let me fly in the azure limitless sky'.
Where crazy winds flow unperturbed, directionless.
Where sauntering clouds make up a dreamland.

Love's not a lie

Suffocate not your love to die.

Let it breathe life, give it space.

Genuine it is, not a lie.

Can see in your eyes, face to face.

Every movement it makes with grace.

Only it needs a patient heart.

Patterns you may easily trace..

That evolves into a master art.

Resilience

At some point, the aligned path goes topsy-turvy.
Overtaken perplexed mind seems more unworthy.
Impassible space, surface betwixt the closest hearts.
Awkward silence reign by the time bound dictates.
Love and intimacy get erased like the evading rainbows.
Unseen forces press on to yield to the coercive blows .
Loathe remains to be the only language to interact.
Innumerable reasons rally to approve the defeat.
Estranged one feels as loose sands slipping off a fist.
Howsoever fragile, those moments too will pass on.
Every cloud has a silver lining is not just said, but done.
Trust in Almighty's will, light can't be veiled for long.
Stay integrated, immune deeper to the soul all along.
Its not just a run, you're the torch bearer to lead.
Count countless others who you precede, succeed .
Everytime fear's beheaded, you march steps ahead.
Neither alone, nor unarmed you're in this battlefield.
The cumulative accretion will pay off the arrears.
Renaissance you will inscribe in golden letters.
Biased inferences will prove baseless, fall off.
Beside you, He is ever there to escort, boost you up.
You have been triumphant, so will you be to the very last.
Either ways victory is a must, as you gave up not in your worst...

Life of a Dandelion

Nay the roses are heavy weighted.
Others too..So bounded to their names.
Bored in self pride, their nemesis.
Display their preposterous facades in vanity.
And emit fragrances to lure every passersby .
No blossom could win over his heart but one.
A life that speaks volumes on ultimate sacrifice.
To the cause of humanity she delivered every bit of her.
And as if it was not enough to her benevolence...
Her sun gave up to moon, moon to stars..
And from these stars emerged countless suns.
The breeze so ardently amores the Dandelion..
How could she have denied!
Extends her hands and yields, gladly severs.
On his wings he takes her off to the land of fantasy..
To let her touch and feel the sky of woven dreams...
May be to far flung lands never imagined..
Or where tiny hands are waiting with open palms.

Conquer over a Quagmire

Brisk, buoyant were you, barely touched the ground...
A poised river you were assured to find a way.
Had to the least envisioned, the dire would surface.
An alien force would command your movement.
A step ahead would claim your sanguineness.
Its when fate's been hideous, stuck you in a quagmire.
Echoes of helpless screams may not get an aid.
Don't seek for the Father...neither for His angels.
Be your own saviour in this self-centred sphere.
Having known the life skills won't serve the need either.
Call upon your intellect, haul it up to kinda perfection.
Even a bullheaded quagmire will quitclaim before you.

Incarcerated

The four walls and the roof overhead ain't secure.
Delineated is my world, delimited my purview.
Forced to obey the extreme rules that I never made.
A window sill, through it I watch a bird flying.
People enjoying freedom of a life, its sweetness.
Today its Sunday..family time and entertainment.
Someone out there loitering the terrace with a pet dog.
Someone watering the drooping plants to revive them.
Somewhere youngsters playing cricket with enthusiasm.
Afar the vehicles honking faintly, people are muted.
My enslaved mind is being betrayed and shackled.
A hostage I'm, left out in the dark dungeon of moira.
I suffer the suffocating, musty odor of a closed room.
Here wind doesn't flow, and the sun does not pass.
Pitter-patter fall of rain does not enchant me anymore.
The otherwise generous moon fail to offer me solace.
Rainbows doesn't make my life any colourful.
Here food tastes bland, water..no water, air..hardly breathable.
Here happiness dare not step, nothing cheers me up.
A hell of a life where my heart burns night and day.
Every moment, the only dying wish is to be emancipated.

Saga of the Fall

The sun-baked, rain-awash guileless hearts..
Survived the wrathful summer, the slashing rain.
Halted not..just in case to complain or regret.
Never ever knew what it means to bloat or burn.
Rather counted moments in years of blessings.
As they lived a wholesome life, seasons across.
Wild or not, endorsed or not, they were mirthful.
And they never sought of due credits to them.
Just ecstatic by themselves being crafted by Him.
Beautified with strokes of heart warming hues.
At twilight, streaks of gold shone through them.
And the fateful day arrives, they must bid adieu.
For what they once took, must return with gratitude.
And relinquish every bit about them in deliverance.
To prostate before the lord for His benediction..
To fall off and litter in subtle sweet surrender.
Rustling psithurism resounding all ears...
Their last signs be like swan song.

Rain drops..Tear drops

Calefaction amplified, feelings pronounced.

Aqua vaporized, sentiments dissipated.

Dense clouds condensed, visceral emotions intensified.

Lightening flashed and thunder rumbled,

Eyes dilated and breaths constrained.

Rain precipitated, brine secreted.

Some rains percolated into the gaea,

Some tears sank into the labrum.

Some rains ran down the slopes,

Some tears rolled down the cheeks.

Fading Hues

Numerous tiny droplets of dew.
Bow of rain that forms so few.
Fog that extends to impair my view.
Blossoms that bloom to die anew.
Short-lived are these ephemerals although,
They give and give and claim the show.
Summer rain vaporizing.
Crepuscule gently evading.
Footprints on sands of time disappearing.
Evanescent memories of a senile fading.
A few such things left with little time to spare.
Some treasured moments are golden and rare.

Alienation

The diminutive mindsets of perpetrating havoc to a reckoned few.
Therein lie masquerades, with sugar coated words they brew.
Their hideous, brazen ridicule over watching the prey stranded.
Consumed by the falsehoods their lives of boastfulness made.
Out of their satanic domain many a wicked witch forays.
And sail off willfully to isolate those marooned castaways.
Their pernicious needled eyes, daggered tongues, devilish grins...
The malevolence that bleeds, amputates the heart into smithereens.

That which endures..

Beyond the conventions of conservative ideas..
Beauty isn't skin deep but deep down to the soul.
Impassioned yearnings emanate pangs of the heart..
To re-unite with love, same as breaths to life.
Apathy rips apart while empathy brings together..
Where profundity of compassion bears a heart.
Souls become inseparable, come what may..
Where love is not humiliated but esteemed high.
Flows with briskness of a river to meet the Sea..
Osculates fervently to be acknowledged as one.
There love resides enduringly where it feels safe..
And guileless hearts persevere the insurmountable.

Break Free !!

If you can shed off the itchy skin that was never yours for sure.

If you can float above your blood carrying chauvinism, selfdom.

If you can break free from stipulated, rigid social norms.

If you can sense the pain of a weeping or silent heart.

If you can untangle a feud with apology and deep felt love.

Then consciously or not...

You have opened the gates of heaven to someone.

And you have given a new life to the one with dying faith.

The age-old patriarchy is debarred at your end...

To starve and die, unfed with prejudiced dark orthodoxy.

A sparkling rebel is borne to lead a thousand successors.

A virgin sun takes off to announce a new dawn.

You may not believe, the gaia is not the same anymore.

Ripples of righteousness from you travel across in the air.

31

A Vaccum

You were once that majestic river, now shifted its course.
Nothing has remained of you since you abandoned us.
Saving those imageries that has remained like a verse.
An accentuated meander forming paleo-ox bow lakes.
Remnants still yearn for the nostalgic bygone days,
Cry out for the stupendous river they were once a part of.
Somewhere you must be now,
Whichever form I do not know.
May be you are an invisible energy afloat...
Or embodied with a certain mass, weight.
I know not whether you have an unquenched thirst...
Or you are in unburdened ease, put to eternal rest.
Had you been signalling me to speak out your heart's rues?
All these time were you all alone only weeping out woes?
Are you there missing me and those beats you left here?
Albeit you so evidently parted, still why I think you're there!
I so badly seek a glance of you but why so all in vain?
May I please meet you by grace of God and when?
Why there is no catharsis for this open agony?
Why moira scathingly bestows it's hegemony?
This bereaved soul be redressed with a soul to soul alliance.
Interacting with her departed soul may I feel her existence..
The unknown force that abruptly delineated our touch,
Is the one that purposedly had once united us as such.
I implore oh God! Give me respite from these hurtful longing tides,
Or else why not take me to that unseen realm where she now resides.

Save a part of you

Times are prone to change with life's upheavals.
People clinging will move far away and disappear..
Akin to stellar bodies in the ever expanding Universe.
Veracity of life will manifest in unanticipated ways.
When you are not prepared to face the worst eventualities.
Life knocks you down badly sans the slightest remorse.
Here, as you seek from within, there will be clarity.
You will get to know the nature, purpose of existence.
Then save the larger hopes in the cauldron of heart.
Let some light enter your soul for those dark, dreary days.
For when your barque sinks, you should be swimming.
Save some weaponry too in the secret chambers...
To fightback a war, all of a sudden declared on you.
And triumph the loosing battle with an inbuilt army.
Save some sunshine smiles and moonlit tear drops.
Strengthen your mind from now to bow not to fate.
Soul will guide, usher you through untrodden paths.

Utopia

No fear of failure...no prospect of pain.
No race of races..no dearth..no disease.
Victory doesn't mean elimination.
No space for arms, ammunition.
No stratification..no disparate fate.
Man, just a fellow being, not a primate.
Not a pinch to satiate greed.
An ocean to serve one's need.
Aversion or rivalry, no sign or trace.
Empathy persuades with a seraphic grace.
Fraternity presides in every humble heart.
Unconditional love is the best known art.
I strive to think the unrealistic,
reality was once a dream.
Greys will be gone one day,
Vacuum infilled to the brim.

Unburden the Childhood

Why the fragile, innocent childhood is drowned in sufferings..
That could not be handled nor shared?
Why immeasurable pains piled up, lay hidden deep within,
But the stable eyes show off?
Why should apprehensions, insecurities rule their tiny world,
Pull them inwards to the abyss?
Why not the childhood be handled with diligence, intelligence,
With due care and unconditional love, sans expectations?
Why not the canvas of those little hearts be painted..
With cheerful and laughing colours?
Why not the angels be so light hearted that they soar..
Higher in the sky of their dreams?

Half a Poet

Can talk of fantasy in utter despondency.
Can sell my dreams in nightmarish reality.
Can make feel paradise out of inescapable hell.
Can taste you sweet liberty in confinement.
Can tell you of peace in total pandemonium.
Can charm you with life, striving disease and death.
In the sandy desert can grow a valley of flowers.
In extreme climes comfort with the Mediterranean.
Amidst vulnerability can bring upon immunity.
Call me a manipulator, a liar.
Its the way I'm, will remain to be so.
I believe to make you believe..
Feathery breaths can sigh away weighty pensiveness.
A glint of aspire can replace dark despair.
My distraught thoughts barely reach you..
Oft they transmute into fortitude.
Innermost notion of my skaldic heart you may never know.
Even not whole, a half poet am I, earnest and callow.

Diverse ways

Some gathered noxious smoke choked my throat as such.
To dispossess that which weighed down, I broke out unashamed..
Brine breaching banks, gushing away unguarded.
Despite encircled by an anonymous crowd..
Saline drops oozing desperately..struggling to bring an equilibria.
Unholy susurrations could be heard loud and distinct.
Uncontained pathos lying unattended..cold and bare.
A comrade's apathy took me by thunderous shock.
Who bore an abhorrence since time unknown.
A warm hug not offered nor exchanged a few words.
Didn't even stand by to pacify the turbulent turmoil.
Seeing me suffer the sadist was exhilarated to the brim..
Misery of one became a source of delight to the other.
I was bypassed, sidetracked sans the least concern.
The preposterous in a hurry to spread over a hot theme.
To rejoice tell tales in a group of malevolent mindsets.
People who boast but never can be anyone's friend.
I parted away to invest my time in a far better way.
Not to breed animosity but to be in peace with self.
We cannot change the world but surely a few with love..
All expertise will fail, however hard we try to get along..
We cannot be everyone's cup of tea, no matter what.

Epiphany

Shrouds of distrust drained me day and night.
Pirates plundered me of my treasured simplicity.
Disarrayed mind played truant time and again.
Was lured to the cliff top only to be kicked off.
Impenetrable, deep seated my agony, left untreated.
Over these years, I desperately searched for a respite.
I sought of it at every possible place in vain.
To my disbelief...now explored a peaceful enclave.
More breathtaking than any dream-like hill resort.
Yep!! I exactly located, its pervasive within me.
'twas ever there by default since day one sans notice.
Only I was blind in the fold of worldly affairs.
The crepuscular rays of the sun have touched me.
And my vista has opened same as a new born's.
Rest assured a perennial bliss to follow lifetime.
Its my shell, my sanctuary, my safe haven.
Herein all kinds of turbulences dissipate, cease to exist.
A bubble where no one can trespass.
To where I retreat when I'm distraught.
I can meditate in composure for its noise proof.
Accords me sanctity from my emotional breakdowns.
Can repair my worn outs through inner engineering.
A rabbit hole it is..to escape into a wonderland.
The deeper I travel, the more I tap the eternal bliss.
Emancipated I feel akin to a bird lost in its flights.

Wanderlust

Burgeoning trepidations jolt me so,
I stumble with a bolt of vertigo.
This wry countenance has lost its sparkle,
An innate grace can revive the dazzle.
Mundanity of quotidian life,
Pushes me to an unbroken strife.
Yearning soul seeking glee for a respite,
Desperate to flee from the serpent's bite.
Fernweh cravings arouse the wild desires,
Raging flames to douse in the joyful tears.

Time's Illusion

Time ticks off unidirectional.

Had it been reversible, things would have been different.

Alas! Should one have rectified regrets, repents.

Burgeoning errs could have been erased, re-written.

Time tricks past-present-future. Pendulum swings memories to and fro dreams.

The now signifying the hanging solid ball.

Rest others, just unrealistic assumptions.

Time tracks the travel path of vibrations.

Evaluates hidden thoughts and open actions.

Weighs and reckons the overall karma.

Rewards with a step up, penalises a step down.

Time's vehicle takes you on an adventure.

A strange time dilation, experienced.

Speeder it's motion, slower the ageing.

Velocity is but relative to another object, static or dynamic.

Awaken to guard yourself

The spiteful arrows thrown at you can't bleed you.
But would recurve right at the aggressor to atone.
Will leave the malevolent perplexed of a failed strategy.
Its when you seek the most significant towards awakening.
Then you would be shielded, not a harm can reach you.
Only if it had touched you, should you have reacted!
There you are..! Blocking the negative energies.
Being nonchalant you accept venom and nectar identically .
Become love yourself, blessed with the seventh heaven.
Clarity in thoughts impart you a strong foundation.
Equilibrium keeps your inner chemistry intact.
Then outside chaos cannot claim your inner peace.
Channelising energies, make you truly empowered.
Nobody else but you are now your own sentinel.
Climb up the foggy mountains of your dreams.
See the minuscules gradually disappear in phases.

Love had been waiting

A thousand tumultuous paths traversed,
No where did I grace the exquisite bloom.
In whose fragrance, would do away with my rues.
And rediscover my hidden blossomed self.
With a heavy heart I sought for it all the way.
Saved myself, walking away from faking fugitives.
At the day's end but defeatedly retreated.
One day..I so chanced upon the unprecedented.
Love's standing by to adorn me in its eternal beauty.
So distinctly distinguishable my intuitions knew.
It would give away to bits without a sigh.

Shh !!

You got me quite a lot but that's not all about me.

Few brimming emotions you haven't ever been through.

From deluging I have had them dammed right away.

They now reside close to my heart..being so honest, being so true, being so blunt and being so forthright.

They are all by themselves, raw and untouched.

And I deliberately keep them to myself, undercover.

In that way I know what I have hidden inside me.

Stoicm is the reason to sanctity of my mind and thoughts.

May be its the same seed out of which I'm manifested.

Everything can't be told, they won't make sense.

Some words loose their essence if ever uttered.

There is an ocean within me, perhaps you do not know.

I dive in it to find my genuine self unaltered and intact.

The Touch

Now we needed him so badly yet he vanished for ever.
When he walked on razors edge, the shrieks didn't reach us.
He lied to us of soft grass beneath his feet.
Smiled roses and sunflowers for he knew just to give.
I seek for his truest love here and there but in vain.
My forlorn heart sobs and sobs as if it will succumb.
Why it had to happen?
Why it had to happen?
Behind me he was standing young and sturdy.
Profoundness of his emotions moulded every heart.
His humility touched the sky.. Godlike his aura.
Why he overtook me to the realm unknown!
Some stabbing questions disturb me often.

Self-Heal

In a surge, life thrashed you badly unprecedented..
And you could not give up living just for your people.
Varied people..varied motifs..varied interests.
However its not them, but altered situations.
The thinned out rope in the tug of war..
At times torn to pieces of threads.
For who renders endlessly is prone to succumb.
It bleeds unstoppable to be taken for granted.
Why not spare some kindness for that deprived one!
The choking piled up pain needs to be cleared.
With a breath of liberty why not date yourself out.
And have an intimate talk, between you and yourself.
Ask of its state, may be by the welcoming Sea side.
A sullen heart would pour out rues..tea from a kettle..
That candid refreshing talk opens up mind's vista..
Be seated at your comfort, feel heaven like serenity.
Treat yourself, a bouquet of honour, love, care.
Introspect on life's wavy ups and downs.
How unwaveringly you had been surfing!
Amidst deadly turns, enough to claim a life.
In this rendezvous with your pious soul..
Watch intently the engaging world around.
Smile to strangers who never gave or took.
Immerse in the overflowing ecstasy of others..
Live the moment, wipe off every bit of remorse.
Laughter mingling with blood.. filling in veins.
Catharsis would happen by nature, en route you.

That mystic seraphim..

When light bids adieu at the eventide,
And shadows of oblivion spreads it's arms.
With a battalion of tiny countless sparks takes over an unfailing companion,
A quintessential of charms.
A wearisome mother sings out lullaby in thy name,
Rocking her infant to restful sleep.
A lone traveller tracks his way,
Thanks thou being not lost in his trip.
I reminisce bygone tidings good and bad,
Seek solace to my bleeding heart's rues.
Perhaps those clouds passing by thy silvery orb,
Whisper to thee of my woes.
A trail of my memories glide across thy placid luminous countenance.
Then something hypnotises me, eyes transfixed, I enter my trance.
As drops of silver pours over,
And soothes into my soul to heal..
I bathe in that elixir,
Inherit some of thine elysian tranquil.

Mirror

Aren't you impersonated,

entitiyless sans your darker base?

So do I emerge, re-emerge from the shattered hopes, I trace.

Bored inside of me, you are that resplendent looking glass.

Through you, I come up across my self, day by day, upon me you so flash.

Those swings of mood as of tides and ebbs.

Those stir of emotions be like tempests and doldrums.

To break through the incongruent norm, I travel...

From cacophonous noises to the serenity of my mind.

My capriciousness and trepidations are hurdles I see, and strive to overcome them.

My falls and failures challenge me, for the indomitable to tame.

Fireflies

Fireflies phosphoresce in the pur blind vision granting a fiery delight,
Imitate the infinite twinkling stars that blink in the pitch black night.
Pulses of luminance as they throw at rhythmic intervals,
My rapturous sprite reverberates waves of ecstatic ripples.
Flashes of Green-Yellow light resurrects the child in me.
In awe I take them in my palms those tiny sparks to see.
Far away from the concrete earth, am I brought forth to some dreamy world?
Or had I been slumbering deep and into my sleep a dream has crawled?
A swarm of you mesmerize me, as hither and thither you fly about.
Whether you are the messengers of God, in my mind I still have doubt.

48

Let's be strangers...

In the surge of time as strangers we met.
Fate lines conjoined to our kismet.
It went like divine wish from eyes to heart's alcove.
From antagonists we kept it safe and reserved.
Stood the ordeal and passed the litmus test.
Overcame the obdurate obstacles to our best.
Smouldered every moment in the fire of separation.
Furnaced love's clay to become strong with emotion.
Our transcendental fervour was coincidental.
Spring tides of longing made us sentimental.
The arrow of Cupid bled through our hearts.
Yet blessed us with the utmost precious.
Love we sought for and aimed and won.
Held the fragile with due care and caution.
To fathom we dived into the dark ocean depth.
Numbed our feelings, there waited freezing death.
We cheated on its face, moved to the surface.
Resuscitated..survived the worst by God's grace.
Let's wade off our limbs as amateurs oh dove!
Let's be strangers once again..let's redeem love.

Love again

Many moons back our hearts alligned together.
Walls grew, repelled us, as we were very near.
Some traits of love long forgotten.
It's about time the unlearnt relearn.
Let's endeavour for lost faith to restore.
Let's not allow our sweetness turn sour.
The cosmos had blithely graced our amore.
Whispers, urges to see it happen ever more.
Some stains can be removed, gaps would cover.
Come a bit closer, make me feel that fervour.
If lament we must, shed a love tear.
Behold me like I am but you my dear.
Vehemently let's waltz to a tune, doused in the rains.
Hands entwined navigate through the sea of pains.
Impassioned, listen to breaths, exuberant.
Unleash the eternal amore, flow incessant.
It's mended! It's done..The bridge to cross.
Our ceaseless affinity will gather no moss.

50

Move on..

Ooze not your tears in the dark.

Accept the reality, even if stark.

Hiding only reveals your core pain.

Howsoever tricks you may plan.

If it persists and burning you, burn it out soon.

Suffer not every moment an uncommitted sin.

If a void is what left in your heart, fill it with love.

Having felt death, live..do the needful and serve.

Regret not for the loss to grieve, God's will prevails is not a lie.

Let slowly die away the deluded ties holding on to which you die.

Dusky Twilight

Fugitive, momentous, sombre, coyish twilight.
Ambles tip-toed from blazing day to nipan night.
Crimson, caramel absorbs shocks 'n stresses.
Encompasses sought after eternal blissfulness.
Bags a load of granny's engrossing stories.
Parades a caravan of nostalgic memories.
A recession from quotidian cyclic tasks.
A revival break for steaming tea 'n snacks.
Homebound avians track their ways back.
Clouds saunter, wind blows with a knack.
Verdant relish cool minty refreshment.
Tender hearted blossoms make merriment.
Artful Silhouettes appear in the growing darkness.
Boisterous world slowly drowns in restful silence.

Me, Myself and I...

I'm not what you form an idea of, mere flesh and blood.

Beyond the mortals, I'm the deathless mind, emotives.

I'm not a possession, you misconstrue as in your control.

You are born to me, I'm the divine Godess in disguise.

I do not deserve your abuses, detest or assault.

For who I'm, I rever myself, that's enough...everything.

I'm not a lone traveller, without you walking along this journey.

Together we're complete, best pals ever..me, myself and I.

Ferris Wheel

Hearts hollowed as we trekked up, screamed with engulfing fear.
Slowly as we reached the pinnacle, distanced from our near ones.
Then fell off free to where we had started just moments before.
Gathered strength to replace fear every time more..much more.
Till heart was left only with courage, fear shown back door.
Did round abouts over and over again and let amusement pour.
They could feel the adventure, who were unbothered, undaunted.
Abstained those who thought it foolishly...they were the fainthearted.

An ode to the Mother...

To my inherent ailments, she is the Jasper stone.
She nourished me right from the day I was born.
Her five elements very much pervasive in me.
Representing the whole, inside a replica I see.
She taught me to be dynamic in life's battlefield.
To defend from the perpetrators, I am my shield.
For ages our men fought for a spark.
In the dungeons but they ended in dark.
To strangulations, gun shots, lathi charge, they succumbed.
Bowed not, curtailed their breaths, for us freedom earned.
Life was then a maze..no means to end, no ends to meet.
They slept by the ominous night and light for us dreamt.
This auspicious day of liberty to write in gold.
To release us from the Imperialists' fold.
My motherland...my faith, in diversity unifies.
In fortitude, in sacrifice the possible limit defies.

Survivance

Above the ineptness is found one's sustain-ability.

Beyond all fuzzy impossibilities lies a crystal possibility.

Surpass inhibitions, determinants one and all.

Right there you are, they call it miracle..

Desolated not, you are the ultimate.

Sprout off the shell in that rocky waste.

With roots of iron incise through the bedded blocks.

Thwart the durability of the so-called resistant rocks.

Forsaken many would wither away to seasonal upheavals.

But you be the testimony of change to deluges and dry spells.

Be the meta person to bear the torch of endless hope.

Seeing your light, a forlorn soul would then not give up.

An aura of sanctity, nimbus encircled.

Paradisiacal benedictions be bestowed.

Flourishes the life, spent on humanity service.

A humble yet dissent life is worth many a lives.

Wish you take me away oh Zephyr..

Each passing day I ponder over your secret errand.
Where it is that you surreptitiously abscond?
And you bring blessed smiles with every return,
Share me how come you're rejuvenated, you're reborn!
Do take me this time oh thou Zephyr,
To the land of utopian dreams, fairytales.
Where less touched is nature, where morn and eve, happiness hales.
Where vales, hills, verdant and firmament, delude of a new born earth.
There I would float and fly by your wings,
the blithesome air to breathe.
From a bird's view, a canopy of thickets I would grace upon.
Your wings will let me descend to the paths, untrodden.
May I then chance upon the wild blossoms,
Where beauty's lost and nobody knew.
And stand by along the levees to watch,
the wild river flow with awe.
Then move to those unknown folks,
cherish their rusty, colloquial talks.
A common thread that communes them,
tied through love knots.
To satiate my thirst, with their crude simplicity I would fill my heart.
Would loiter upon the enriched soils,
soothe them gently with my hands.
And through you, by 'Petrichor' I would be known.
As you are loved, I too will bag some love back home.

When love speaks

Eyes furled, meet me neath the unloved tresses.
Barren my heart, wrap me in your cosy embrace.
Bonfire is lighted to warm your frozen bosom.
Fall for me like hailstones, only to melt thereupon.
Collect me so like a fragile glass, lest I may break.
Exchange words of silence, hearken lub-dub speak.
Waltz to the rhythm of my every smitten breath.
Lost in sweet harmony let's obliviate this earth.

Ultimate Tranquility

When faking colours will fade away..
My genuine self will emerge.
When pomp n show will be called off..
That silence will be my say.
When self ego will loose the battle..
I will be my dignified self.
When things that matter, won't anymore..
A vacuum will I embrace.
When conundrum will uplift it's obscuring veil..
My trajectory will be enlightened.
When I seek to know of my existence..
Material interests will become immaterial.
Thereby I will be wholesome, sans timid desires.
Then I will be at the pinnacle of eternal tranquility.

Let your love live

Its not always the other..
Why play the blame game !
He may be truest at his place.
You may be honest to the core.
Still things go amiss as you cannot get along.
Oh no..its not love-hate, nor it is pure hate.
Situations do juggle between best and worst.
Feuds n fights pop up, as heated temper burns.
A paradise may turn into a battleground..
When you are blind to him and he is deaf to you.
You need to wear his shoes..
To chisel your senses a bit.
And subside and contemplate..
To bring the best in you.
Then you will find..love is not dead yet.
But it's you and him who are smothering it.
A day lost never returns, time fleets by.
Squeezing memories will do no good.

Dream Catcher

A thing of charm, hangs from the wall, next to me.
Hues imbibed feathers, hand-crafted artistically.
A prelude to slip into an orchestra, thus initiates.
Gentle breeze blow the light feathers slight off place.
Cradled breaths, swing to the ethereal beauty.
Somnolent eyes dive deep, fall off now and again.
Akin to the dark clouds saturate...condensate.
Neurons rush as messengers to the body and brain.
A Shadow takes charge over the conscious mind...
To disown the weariness to the Goddess of sleep...
To drown in a sweet, serene slumber..to catch a dream...

Nobody cares

That frail child too was carried nine months in womb..
And for years together loved close to the heart.
Alas! Had to go through a painstaking ordeal.
Famished eyes, begged of life in the form of a morsel.
Mercy played truant when the kid was starving.
How come the surroundings became so cruel !
Hard to believe, none caught sight of the child..
How could the so-called closed ones give up !
Or they didn't press hard for their right to live !
Ultimate silence won the game on easy terms.
Someone's jewel, worth nothing to anyone.
There goes the saying..children are everyones'..
Do we really reflect upon them as our own!
Self-absorbed people would hardly pay heed to those around..
Lives are circuitous, empathy to a fellow, extraneous
Posh villas, five star hotels, aristocracy..mocked aloud.

The End

As the last drop of kindness exhausted..
Chaotic madness at its peak replaced benignity.
What a brainless race for non-existent pseudo power!
Death reigned in barbarous bloodsheds.
From choking smoot, marooned her rose to find nothing.
Flattened her haven and neighbourhood.
Her rosy soft feet had never before tasted dust..
Her small sized belly could not make out hunger pangs.
And now the disaster was dumped on her altogether.
The Apocalypse left her traumatised..panic stricken.
This disorder..that spared her life and left her dead.
Losing family was loosing self..undeniably unacceptable.
Pitiful eyes peeped out through the smoky reality.
Humanity was lost amidst bullets and bombs.
She remained stunned, paralysed, blanked out.
In the aftermath she never thence spoke a word.

Deluge

The goblet was remorselessly pouring out fire.
And I was terribly pulling down..contracting in girth.
My burgeoning laments were building up.
A passive part of me I so wished to get rid off.
Rues lifted..switched to form fluffy floaty clouds.
Warm ties had long withheld those saline drops.
And all at once the chilly-cold air blew me up.
I burst open my bag of painful belongings.
Gave way to unprecedented torrential rain.
Renamed..an untamed river in umpteen spate.
Swelling...over spilling the riparian edges.
Unannounced made my way..gushing in a flash.
Breaking apart..artificial dykes..
Bankfull..I flowed with cadence.

'AUM'...The Sound of Black Hole

An omnipresent sacred sound encapsulates the cosmos.

An omnipotent subtle energy pervades the totality.

An omniscient sublime consciousness, harmonizes the macrocosm.

'Aum'..with it's variants, 'Ameen', 'Amen', evoke divine energy.

Energy, that aligns the chakras(wheels) to flow unblocked.

The rainbow of seven chakras open to cosmic unity.

This root mantra (chant) connects to Ajna chakra, 'the third eye'.

Brings upon self knowledge, intuition and relaxation.

Reverberation of the chant makes one with the Universe.

The mind meditates to grace the supreme absolute.

Travels from Maya(illusion of the reality) to transcendental state...

From materialism to spiritual awakening...

From worldly desires to no desires.

Aspects of time, space, consciousness attains unity.

Loose their meaning to the black hole of nothingness.

Everything tangibles become non tangibles in a puff.

Accentuated existence with its drowning questions...

Simplified with the primordial sound of creation.

The big bang event replays itself, fills the mental vacuity.

The Sky is red

I guessed a different mood of the firmament.
Blood had splashed across to its far end.
This day it doesn't reflect upon the tranquil sea.
But the troubled waters fested with storms.
It's disarrayed thoughts would climb the surging waves.
It's rebellious mind is not upto obeying nature's order.
And it is dancing with all its vigour and passion.
Restless..flawless..un sceptical..unhindered.
Daring to rise above mundanity, mediocrity.
Outbursting, breaching the controlling borders.
Rulling out..expanding..oblivious of it's own limitations.
Breaking the norms, trespassing the binding laws.
Splendour, that crossed the barriers of thoughts...
Transgressed to glorify the lot, far and away.

Soul Connection

Every element, your soul is made up of..
There someone knows with such dexterity.
Had been reading it..since aeons ere..
Perhaps you would hardly imagine.
The span of time that elapsed by then.
Divinity conspired..stars fell into a pattern.
How destiny links up paths once crossed!
Ages melting in preserved moments.
An unconscious prolonged wait, worthy too.
Ah! A long long search..lastly you were figured out.
No matter what..the soul, the aura is same.
Smiling eyes..guarding you of potential hazards.
Endearingly adoring your empathy and enlightened ways..
Along it, you taking your mind holding its fingers.
Your hard earned humility enchants someone.
And you stop being possessive about your heart.
It becomes raw, indefinite with deluging emotions.
Two lonesome poetries seamlessly merging into one.

Lights in the dark

Sky rocketing sparkling lights,
a triumph declare..
Malevolent shadows be drowned by veracity, just n fair.
Lamps of burning hope pacing through the dense air.
To reap as is sown and to each his own share.
The aligned oil dipped wicks gently catching fire.
Obeisance to the five elements off an earthenware.
At a distance, akin to stars twinkle many a flare.
Take a firm stand with an oath, to make aware.
A solemn consensus, of peace to prevail everywhere.
Illumined dreams to take over oblivious nightmare.

Nishabd

The superficial five senses, body and mind becomes inane...
Its when life energy penetrates from surface to core (sounds to soundlessness).
Reverberations become pointless, cease to exist ...
Its when the entire creation resonates in tandem.
The cycle of Karma breaks to enlighten the entirety...
Its when the point of Moksha (Salvation)is attained by one and all.
There is end to sufferings arising out of desires.
Its when the state of absolute bliss is reached.
Light radiating out get absorbed into its source.
Its when the exhausted, duty-bound time rests in solace.
Nishabd is not only Naad (silence)..its that state where there is..
No life..
No death..
No creation..
No creator.

Sanatana Dharma

The laws of eternity wherein religions dissolve.
Walls of self-imprisonment collapse and fall.
Barriers of conservative faith lifted...
Impositions, restrictions called off.
Individual interests, immediate needs given up.
Where love flows free into one another.
Where longing is to expand limitless.
All these for the greater order of things in unison.
A supreme law abridges across all life processes.
Wherein the body and soul becomes one with God.
And mind is not enslaved by fear or threat, but liberated.

Besos de amore

You tended my covert aches all through the years.
Marooned me not, shielded me from stress shears.
Yet all, time and space had us depart.
Grow your longing, sew the rip apart.
Like those weary eyes at once you read.
And swerving breaths you keenly heard.
My inflamed gores would soothe to heal.
My benumbed senses will sense and feel.
Partake with me a passion fruit, that's pure.
For life long whose sweetness would linger.

"Women Empowerment: World Empowerment"

Why conceal behind the curtains and closets, Oh woman!! you're the pride.

The Sun you are, not secluded, that radiance how can you confide?

How broken or devastated you may be, search out for a spark.

Gather the shards of your heart, with vigour anew to fight back.

A serene river you are, no obstruction can ever hinder your path.

Flow then unstoppable, unwarranted, emancipated, Oh holy faith!!

Not a commodity you are to be sold in exchange of a supportive price.

A giver you are so deserve the best, soar high and rise.

Never underrate those virtues that you have in store.

Emotions make you, with it your benevolence an elixir.

Your eyes, touch and voice filled with affection, replete with grit.

Beauty isn't skin deep but beyond...it defines your tender heart.

Break all shackles of fakeness that bounds you to captivate.

No power is that enough to subdue your divine state.

You are not in a race to compete, a counterpart of man you are.

Not a pawn of someone's shrewd move, a game changer you are.

Every pain or agony passing through toughens you, makes you more stronger.

You grow to equip with circumstances, facing a fear or danger.

Set your life's goals to reach out for your aspired dreams, march forward.

Incredible, invincible come victorious with time and space conquered.

You are complete in yourself in every manner, the cosmos in your fold.

You are the omnipotent Goddess Shakti, the protective cover of the world.

When things are tangled and out of order you lubricate, make it easy going.

You are the pillar of relationships, under your shade life keeps growing.

Time and again it is true, as you are empowered the world is too.

Parijata

Oh heavenly wonder why bloom thou so in the lonesome night..?

With freshness of life amaze me with thine incense delight.

My eyes still, breaths unswerving..

Oh ! thou alluring Parijata, may I grace upon thee.

A soulful of thou would take in and out, my sedative senses to awaken and free.

Thine intoxicating fragrance would rush into every nook and corner of me.

To partake my worries thou chance upon, all memories fade, I think of thee.

In Twilight thou gleam and sparkle with an enigma more as even dew.

An elysian bliss, how one can deny, such auspicious glimpses count so few.

As you make fall, with splendour thou deliver thine self to the earth.

Oh thou epitome of Pulchritude!! My gloom's effortlessly consumed to mirth.

Evanescent thou art called so, but thine indelible impact can I forbear?

An undying crave lingers in me..'To seek for you'..It lives in me forever.

73

Freedom

Freedom is the name of a bird, flying stupendously, above man-acclaimed territories, hopes manifesting.

Freedom is the name of a river, flowing magnificently, quenching thirst of souls, beyond discriminating.

Freedom is the name of that wind, blowing tremendously, relieving lives reeling under the scorching heat.

Freedom is something that transcends a cage, an obstruction, a barrier to excel that feat.

For me it is to be myself composed, poised, deep down to the soul.

To have my self-ordained rules, none so there to dictate me, play foul.

Where I'm safe with myself.

Indulge in thoughts that are my very own.

Where I'm the master of my inner premises.

None so there to harm, affect or intervene.

Where not a thing restrains, enslaves, weighs me down.

Where I could go outlaw to speak, act fearless on my own.

Or sometimes, I would go astray somewhere, planned, unplanned.

Loose myself in things, ruminate, cherish and be keenly observant.

Rejoice the company of the self with glee.

Dwell in tranquil that subsides in me.

Nurture, caress, heal...find my niche.

My world of peace.

My space.

Priceless...

Priceless are the non-tangibles,
untagged, non-materials.
Priceless are the perennial, profuse, free gifts of nature,
With its inexhaustible five elements in abundance.
Be it the mellifluous music of song birds,
Mesmerizing shades of rainbows, butterflies, blossoms.
Smile with a consciousness of the breath you're blessed with..
for every bit of existence of life in itself is priceless.
Obstacles be your stepping stones,
Adversaries blessings in disguise.
Your perseverance to surpass them is priceless.
The firmament had been looking for you.
Fearless open your wings, soar higher.
Your larger dreams charged with passions are priceless.
May you know the worth of genuine love, family, friendship,
Foundation stones of a beautiful architecture is priceless.
Behold the virtues of honesty, simplicity, compassion, altruism.
For they are truly the treasures of gold and priceless.
Your freedom of thought and actions,
Your chain of entangled emotions,
Your galaxy of mind and imaginations,
Your perfections in your imperfections,
Are all but virtuals yet priceless.

If I had it my way...

I would have empowered the vulnerables, the voiceless.

Ages of nuisances they bore, they must act, have a say.

Ethics, principles make leaders, though lesser knowns were they.

He can serve equanimity best who did bear the brunts, who did once fall prey.

Lofty heights of vainglory would have tasted dust.

Perpetrators would have shivered with dread.

Unshielded would have found an umbrella overhead.

The day of judgement would not have been a dream far away.

Delivering justice, fast-track-mode would have been the resolve each day.

Then I would have prioritised the marginalised ones,

Would have done all my best for some lost smiles to repay.

Scores would not have validated sagacity.

Self-centeredness would not have certified sanity.

Enlightenment would have meant effortless integrity.

Being human the righteous path would have been paved with humility.

Sacrifice, loyalty would have been the cornerstones,

For truth and justice to prevail all the way.

In lieu of whatsoever this world would have had to pay.

All, but if only, I had it my way.

The symbolism of Unalome

A divine Unalome very few could decipher
In this rivalled cut throat race of life
How lengthened it is with egotic-materialism
How shortened with selfless-altruism
A trajectory only if one could surmise
And the inner light that removes all ambiguities
Where wealth or education are not the yardsticks of spiritual well being
Where humanity is the wealth,conscience the omnipotent knowledge
that reigns
If one could assess how far he is from the ultimate reality
The shortcuts he would resort to, the destination to reach on time
Then he would not dig out trap holes for his fellow men
Rather bury those manholes with his own muscles and bones
If once and for all he acknowledges the cryptic spirals that entangle
He would follow a straight line path to enlightenment
Maintain and polish his roads to travel smooth
Grooming his thoughts and actions that define him

Doll's House

The Doll's enchanting like Cinderella....
Little did for her cascades of serpentine tresses.
Less like for her ocean deep pair of sharp eyes.
Not quite for her succulent, petal-like fuller lips.
Rather for her guileless heart, so rare as it was...
That bore colossal burden and wrath.
Metamorphosed from coal to diamond.
Stood out in sparkle and resistance...
As she smiled through her every pain or sorrow...
With honey's sweetness and purity galore.
Revered every soul and abhorred none.
Returned all detest with pious love.
Cared as though all belonged to her.
Spared not a thought for herself, a tad bit.
Some wistful waves continually pounded up the shore.
That solemn desire grew, a castle to make for her.
A citadel it would be overlooking the milieu.
Bizzare dreams woven with dream filled eyes.
Efforts integrated, labour intensively pulled.
The foundation, the pillars, all sturdily inbuilt.
It's bowed up ceiling held like inverted Noah's ark.
A majestic chandelier hung right from the centre.
The decor was done with incredibly fine artistry.
Pink silken drapery drop endorsed every wall.
Cobblestone paved out on the court yard.
Bushy flora, fruit trees lined up the entrance.

A pond with a fountain where swans waded.
The castle was one resplendent master piece...
In finesse, in grandeur was impeccable.
Alas!! Alike her pair of elegant glass shoes ...
The walls and roofs too were made of glass.

Balmy Silence

The emptiness, audacity of malicious gossips you let me know.

Only then could I make out your fullness, to words that lost their meaning.

I sought for you by looking inside and hearing my own heart to relive yet again.

Oh !! How blessed you are to imparting solace in seclusion sans a fanfare.

I repelled from boastful talks of egomaniacs, since felt uneasy, looked imbecile.

You kept me safe from the malevolent with hidden pernicious intents.

So I unidentified myself with conservatives, materialists, egoists.

My aura clashed, I felt disdained in the midst of groupism, separatists, malignants.

When I was unwanted, unsolicited, I diverged away, being the odd man.

Then your subtle hands caressed me fondly to alleviate my bruised soul.

In my oblivion, I got from you the tender motherly touch that be calmed my mind.

The disruptive sounds I got rid of as I willingly distanced myself away, faraway.

All noises and chaos subsided, drowned as I entered your paradaisical haven.

You spoke to me the kindest way and empathised with my lonely soul till eternity.

Those enriching moments of tranquil outweighed all the worldly pomp and show.

An aura of alacrity kept me surround I received serenity, I attained nobility.

The devouring pain

Shackled excruciating agonies,
Confined in the dungeons of heart.
Outcry aloud for its release,
Alas! To give ears, none took part.
The lurking insider, that parasite,
Ruthless, consumes bite after bite.
Not a drop or trace of crimson,
Still aches pervade deeper albeit.
Bruised bosom, shredded sprite.
Suffering exceeds indefinite.
Valiant breaths, dreaded.
Wholesome life, fragmented.
Fiery eyes, flooded.
Regressive angst, spearheaded.
Desperate self seeks a shoulder,
To shed off, but to no avail.
Helpless...shoulders its head on its own,
To ameliorate, to condole.

The day of a knight

Alongwith the dawn a challenging voyage begun,
With the chorus of some birds and the rising sun.
A sturdy built, an upright posture with the head and eyes held high that kills.
Was it the knight riding the stallion on the windy road running the uphills?
Moving the west won't bring him death,
For the sun had promised with holy faith.
The stars would sure guide the way,
All evils would fall till the doomsday.
The deep seated chivalry, the muscles of iron, the warm blood.
Unstoppable was the solemn warrior all poised and armed.
He then took to the wavy river side that moved in various bends.
The vast stretch of the moorlands, the desert and the wilderness.
While passing by the caravan who were the wayfarers?
A band of gypsies clinging to a bonfire and the traders.
Light fleeted...Dusk and twilight then a dreary night.
The world was in slumber deep, all voices died outright.
His sword shined in the moonlit night like a thunder bolt.
The horse's hoofs raking the hilly tracts toot-toot...toot-toot.
He steadily moved on with austerity crossing the rolling uplands, the rugged mountainous terrains.
How venturesome was he to survive one and every hardship that arrived, rather took all the pains.
The weather's tempest and the press of the storm.
The untamed, unfriendly nature was quite a phantom.
The serpentine river was a torrent.
The trees were unobeying turbulent.

The moist, chilly winds sinking down the vales had many a quivers sent.
His struggle wasn't yet over.
His motif was not at all clear.
His secret errand no one knew.
A brave heart, a prodigy.
He was one among those few.
The rigidities of nature though he had surpassed,
But not yet the rigidities of man.
And then he fought valiantly though single handedly,
All the way from fair to tan.
Till not a resistance stood by his way any further.
Till he bathed with his sweat and blood together.
Till he liberated some men from bondage with very faint chance.
Till the day somewhere a messiah outshone the sun in radiance.

Musical waves

The graceful moves of sound, lilting to the rhythmic beats of the heart.
Ascends like blebs of glassy lava caught in the air, as Pele's hair.
Falls like the rhapsodic rain, overflowing from the saturated clouds.
With such careen it flows like a light footed, mischievous juvenile river.
Riveting..!! Those sonorous strokes sync with the body and soul.
Travels rather gushes into the veins and arteries, suffuses every cell.
Magnetic it's aura, electrifies the being, illumines, magnifies the astute.
That cadence accords the incoherent thoughts a sublime harmony.
It's also a song, the lyrics, modulation of tones that obliterates the greys.
That euphonius ambience encircling becomes catharsis to an aching sprite.

Mind to Soul Talk

As this world sheds off water colours, lend me a shoulder in my blues.
When the burgeoning agonies overtake me, to you I will speak my rues.
Will you then whisper into my ears, the lightness of the kindest hearts?
Will you be that aurora to me and kindle an urge when light departs?
Will you then hold my hand in yours, console to love me till the last?
Will you bring a smile to my lips, bolster to get over my haunting past ?

Mother I'm indebted..

Little did I realise that I too have a paradise.

Will have nothing left sans your shade overhead.

Traces will I blindly seek here and there to no avail.

Fugitive times how I wish to never never end.

Your frail, inept body taking a toll of me more than you.

How you shielded us from every ravaging tempest..

As if you negotiated to take it on you and spare us.

From your safe harbour gleeful we did set sail..

With pomp n' show to destinations unknown.

We left you far behind in our zeal to reach no where.

My pillar of success needs me to lead now.

Your decades of breathless strife bore fruit.

Sleepless nights gave us a relaxing sleep.

Half your hunger filled our stomachs.

Pardon me when I loosely took you for granted..

Mistook or doubted your pious intention.

You were never wrong..a mother can never be.

My moist eyes cannot fathom your truest love.

The Child in me

This long isolation has crippled my limbs.
The child in me peeps with lifeless eyes..
Through the bars of caged beliefs.
With pitiful eyes pleads to be liberated.
So many years passed, passersby crossed..
None cared to give a patient ear to my suppressed grief.
Outgrown frame only augmented the misery.
Yes! I have grown just outwardly.
Its just a natural process.
How could I have stopped it!
But if you care to observe...
I'm the same innocent and a bit pampered child.
One who wondered super men are awesome.
I was bestowed with super powers to manoeuvre.
Over the years my heart remained all the same.
I couldn't learn to take tears.
I couldn't express whatever I feel.
And when you are mad at me..
I have to deal with unmanageable fear.
Deep down I'm still fragile, vulnerable.
Please don't polish or discipline me.
But allow me break rules that restrict.
I'm better in my unrefined state.
Carefree I would fly like a bird.
Unrestrained, flow like a brook.
I just don't want to miss a second.

But to make the most out of life..
Live every moment as if a dream.
With bursts of laughter and joy.
Do you claim to understand me?

If I be..

If I be an absorbing story in your bosom's alcove..
Reserve me for an empath who poured out love.
If I be a music from your mellifluous air..
From the core would I bring sweet nectar.
If I parallel your way of life, line of thoughts..
Would I flash upon you despite all obstructs.
If I be an alteration in your perceptions..
Would I transform gracefully alike seasons.
If I be a glint of hope in your dark despair..
Would I keep kindling to light up your desire.
If behind your furled eyes I be your reverie..
Would we discover our world of phantasmagory.

Grace

In loosing if you could still win the game.
Cherish a rival's victory to the fullest.
As if it were you who made it to the finish line.
Then and there you become invincible.
Neither eyes or skin, nor attire or accent.
Its the soul deep within that shows off.
Nothing in this world can debar you then.
Your transformation is real..
A chrysalis to a butterfly.
A winged beauty with vibrant colours.
Eyes glow more, smile lights up the gloom.
A woman encapsulated in a worshipped diva.
Walks down the hall of fame..With no vanity but pure grace.

Blossoms

Time arrives on tip toe, departs unnoticed.
Ethereal blooms thus become immortals.
Oh !They don't close their petals before time.
Tenderness, sweet fragrance, their ipseity.
Greet with resplendence, beautifying a day .
Spread solace, with such ease exchange love..
Vales, river banks, meadows impassioned.
A life so simple, blissful by Divine creation.
Vivacious, they grace enriching lives flourish.
This miraculous enormity, it's magnificence.
Humbled being a part of the mesmerising collage somewhere.
Everso gratifying being assigned a minor role play of a healer.

Being a mother...

Tender childhoods one before, the other after you.
Soft like the dawning and the dusking twilight.
You as a woman at your zenith stand amidst them.
They need your safe hands to cross the roads of life.
Your unfailing shade may never forsake them.
A mother you are to your progeny and progenitor.
Bear up with their constant naggings, mischiefs.
They make you restless still let them sleep with peace.
Forgo your craves and desires to satiate theirs instead.
Be content to let them have your share of ice cream.
Their words may be broken, flawed, unspoken.
Read their psyche with all your heart's perfection.

The Human Chain

Lest we awake the Empath in each one of us...
It will sleep..sleep..sleep to pass away one day.
Lest we appraise ourselves of an altruistic urge..
It won't move an inch nor to that effect lift a finger.
Lest we tickle our grey cells, commune a motif..
It won't assess the paramountcy of our existence.
Counted few chose paths devoid of material gain.
Had rest others realised, its humane that counts!
The road may be strewn with shards of edgy glass.
Per se devalued..a promising career to sure success.
An Empath may be localised but never isolated.
The reverberation goes with like minded people.
Albeit incognizant, aligns with a multitude others.
An unbreakable chain that goes around the world.

Paradoxy of you and me

If you are me and I'm you,
And I am everyone I see or not...
Then why do I despise myself?
When I should have loved me endless.
And why do I'm jealous of me?
When I should have been blissful always.
Why I'm complex with self?
When that simple is the ultimate truth.
We all are sparks of the same Supreme Power.
There is divine oneness all around the cosmos.
Varied reflections, karmas, frequencies, wavelengths...
Split one identity in numerous ways, slacken the spritual progress.
I'm that killer...the victim too I'm.
I'm the warden...the prisoner
I'm a man...a woman also.
I'm a protozoa...a metazoa.
I'm the sun...the rain.
I'm the stream...the sea.
I'm the dust...the ash.
I'm everywhere...pervading space.
I'm immortal, I happen till eternity.

91

Driftwood..

Once I made a majestic tree, stood tall and strong.
When I was logged out, knew not where I was upto.
Soon I encountered the sea, the very first time.
I was sent by my stars to be with the wavering waves.
Hearken their unheard heart, that none pays a heed.
The lonesome vast expanse of the sea, to spare time.
Then sense oscillating curly waves, susurrating.
Their gleeful crests, distressful troughs tumbling down.
And those circular motions, hypnotising angular stones.
Transforming into well-rounded pebbles, cobbles, boulders.
Where I thought was lost, I instead found myself.
As I drifted along, in my ruins and became whole again.

Earth Day

Must be something special that I feel being flanked by.
In this gruelling summer heat, few hands watered me.
My parched mouths assimilated them instantaneously.
Most grateful..they thought about me for a while..
Atleast they acknowledge I too have a life..and can feel love or pain.
They tied a green ribbon..as a token of our friendship.
Nothing I missed..even caught the waves of a song.
These are pure souls..not like those heartless brutes.
I hear..my folks being mercilessly slashed out very often.
Cannot even save my community from the sacrilege..
Regretful and helpless as I'm all at the same time.
We are here for a cause..We are here to save lives.
Can bear the sweltering sun, the thrashing rain..
Only if your prosperity wouldn't be at our cost.
The one who conquers cannot win over hearts..
If you so please our communion would be harmonious.

93

Innate drive

There instantly I identified..
For I knew not to ignore.
My whole body did shake..
As I shook hands with fear.
It whispered into my ear..
The deepest secret ever.
To me drew a line, veneer.
Asked if I could cross over.
And when I touched the line..
It was electrifying.
I thought the fatal shock would take a toll of me..
And I reverted every time.
Lastly I figured out, the jerk was to testify me..my integrity.
Had I that high volt energy!
Were I converged to a point!
I crossed it then..And crossed over and again.
For me it became a way of life.
And I meet fear everyday.
But it has to stay back.
I have to go way beyond.

Cryptic

Ends untraceable..crux unfound..undisclosed book.
Unsurmised sealed off hearts..barely open for a look.
Words ambiguous..become unreachable.
Zip locked lips..emotions unfathomable.
Superimposed thoughts..messy..disordered.
Withered certitude..desolated..unushered.
Undeciphered enigma..shrouded in mysteries enfold.
Cocooned enclosure..shielded in sufferings untold.
Tangled gossamer..spider entrapped.
Blurred vision..dreams far fetched.

Been through Heaven by Happenstance

A momentary epiphany of serendipity,
When blissfulness was at its extremity.
Into nothingness, beyond mortality,
Time froze, became one with eternity.
That divine touch so subtle yet indelible,
In ecstasy, throbbed the heart, palpable.
The soul knew it all at first instance,
As tears outburst in exuberance.
A feel that shook me off, landed me on cloud seven.
For sure, I had been through the gates of heaven.

Rain and Romance

A hectic day, all work no say, love at bay.
Eventide, had some strategies confide.
Blanketed night..episodes of thunder and light.
Soothing, splashing rain on the window pane.
Cool, crispy breeze, oxytocin release.
Straying eyes meet, waves amore hit.
Flickering flame, burning desires to blame.
Impregnated wishes, titillating kisses.
Ecstasy atops..Time stops..

Shades of love

The air is not always pink phantasmagory.
Oh its not a child's throwing tantrums.
Mature love is one that evolves in its truest sense.
Needs a deeper perception of its various shades.
That which is transcendental and caring.
That which is forgiving and forbearing.
That doesn't boast of a bonding, quintessential.
That should essentially mean quint not a controlled trial.
Parted souls, crazy longings and that heavenly meet.
At times smells hatred but then becomes the opposite.
The cacophonous chaotic house seems to be on fire.
A soft breeze takes over, God knows from where.
The world is vigorously shaken up to a disaster's call.
And everything falls right at their places next to the brawl.

Falling in love

As if the eager him had been awaiting aeons long...
Holding on to his best only to deliver those emotions.
And he wells up the much gathered, suppressed amor...
Knowing the burning gaia will value those pearl drops.
To make life he verily falls for love's ascension.
Delves into her parched, deep cracks, the aching gores...
To heal with his divine touch, to soothe and becalm.
Laves her dull and dusty body to refresh, rejuvenate...
To wipe away her harrowing recalls of withstanding the ire.
Plays his resonating, seasoned romantic music, pitter-patter...
To enchant her yearning ears and her lovelorn heart.
Sinks deeper into her saddened, agonised, silenced soul...
And to turn her euphoric, energetic, leaves no stone unturned.

Autumnal Fervour

I was striding along the alley of oak and maple trees.
Coy leaves were whispering love with the wild breeze.
Ruska hues had painted the landscape saffron, scarlet, rusnet.
Sun burnt crispy leaves had fallen to drape the land in auburn raiment.
With every tread, psithurism ignited flames of love's passion.
And serendipity lend the soul a subtle, sublime reverberation.
Charmed, enthralled, mesmerized by the mosaic, kaleidoscopic patterns.
Enigmatic serene charisma illumined the soul to glow like many a lanterns.
A bright testimony of change, the forswearing fall.
Shed its beauty yet came out to be much more graceful.